I'm Worried About Your Drinking

JUDITH MATTISON

Foreword by

VERNON JOHNSON

AUGSBURG Publishing House
Minneapolis, Minnesota 55415

I'M WORRIED ABOUT YOUR DRINKING

Library of Congress Catalog Card No. 77-84093

International Standard Book No. 0-8066-1620-2

MANUFACTURED IN THE UNITED STATES OF AMERICA

for

Pastor Jim Martin
who helped me understand
Doctors Bob Olson and John Lyons
who didn't mince words
Jim D. and the millions of alcoholics
who have been there
and Ann, who knows what it is
to love an alcoholic and survive

Foreword

The first impression one has of this little book is how very poignantly and accurately Judie Mattison presents the emotional plight of those who live with an alcoholic. The bewilderment and frustrations are made clear. "Why doesn't he (or she) see what is happening and quit drinking?" With deeply moving words, the author expresses the hurt and resentment caused by the apparent carelessness and the antisocial or destructive behavior of the suffering alcoholic. The guilt and shame caused by the alcoholic's unconscious projection of his own self-hatred on those around him, the fear and dread resulting from the inability to predict the alcoholic's behavior and to accept responsibility are so clearly presented that all who live with suffering alcoholics will readily identify themselves on page after page.

The deeper, and perhaps more subtle, impression, however, needs to be underlined. Namely, how all these negative emotional reactions serve to enmesh the "co-alcoholic" into similar self-defeating patterns of behavior; how these people become inadvertent "enablers" actually and increasingly contributing to the problem, rather than providing answers for it; how they react rather than act; and how in the end they see the problem "out there" rather than within themselves. These are the most poignant passages.

We can see how, at the very least, those who live with alcoholics are progressively immobilized by their emotional reactions and come to believe they can do nothing to help themselves, the situation, or the alcoholic. As the alcoholic moves inexorably toward premature death, there is only anguish and despair.

It is to be hoped that the impact of this book will allow those living with the alcoholic to recognize not only the plight of the alcoholic, but also their own, and to move from misunderstanding and immobilization to acceptance and action.

VERNON E. JOHNSON, D.D.
President, Johnson Institute

Introduction

On Tuesday, Jim didn't come home from work until well after dinner—and he was drunk. Mary never knew if the children could tell when Jim had been drinking. She tried to conceal her anger and disappointment.

She had hoped that when he left his desk job and began working outdoors he would change. He'd left all those pressures behind. But after work Jim found his buddies in the bars, regardless of the job he held. Even when he was temporarily unemployed, he occasionally "hung one on."

This week he was late four or five workdays and he arrived at a family celebration bleary-eyed, much to the distress of his parents. By Sunday Mary found herself ready to leave for a visit at her aunt's house, to show Jim she would no longer stand for his behavior. They could barely pay bills as it was. Her frustration was acute.

But Mary never left. The next day she talked

to Jim when he was sober. Jim responded well. That evening he was home on time, relatively cheerful, and he was responsible for days afterward. Mary's anxiety was relieved.

Mary's sister encouraged her to talk with a professional counselor or a well-informed pastor about Jim's drinking. Perhaps such a person could advise her about what to do if Jim resumed his drinking. "No," said Mary, "I couldn't do that. I can't accuse him that way. He's much better now. He's practically a new man."

Ralph is a long-time employee of a growing business firm. Though he earns a good salary, he is always in financial difficulty. People like Ralph. He is good-natured and hardworking, and he loves his family. But Ralph's friends at work observe that his lunch breaks grow longer and longer.

Afternoons, his secretary shies away from the smell of liquor on his breath. She has worried about Ralph for some time, and in an effort to help him she has carried more and more of his work load—covering for his absences, apologizing to clients, writing extra letters.

His appearance is unchanged, though, and few people have ever seen Ralph drunk. He can "really hold his liquor," they say. So no one has said anything to Ralph or his boss. But the friends talk among themselves.

"Gee, I'm worried about Ralph. He drinks a lot."

"Let's face it, a lot of business gets carried out over a drink."

"We all have a drink with him when we're out for lunch."

"Yeah, and he holds it so well. I've never seen him drunk."

"I think he has lots of bills, though."

"Well, that house of theirs is expensive. His kids are getting older now too."

"Do you suppose he's an alcoholic?"

"Well, I'd sure hate to say that. He's a great guy. He doesn't look like an alcoholic. I mean, all of us drink—and we're not alcoholics."

"He really isn't working like he used to. His poor secretary. . . ."

"But he needs his job now more than ever."

"I'll tell you one thing. I'd sure hate to bring it up to him."

Esther, a middle-aged woman of upper-middle income, is facing an emptying nest. Her youngest child is a sophomore in college. With this dramatic change in her life, she feels lonely and impotent. She is finding alcohol a good companion.

Ken, her husband, keeps hoping Esther can make it through. Occasionally he scolds and argues. For the most part, he hopes that tomorrow will be different. He avoids social occasions involving Esther and conceals her problem. He suggests new interests to her, but she continually promises and then shrugs when she cannot rise to the occasion.

Jim, Ralph, and Esther are not fabrications. They are live, loving, and hurting people. They are wrestling with chemical dependency.

But they have in common unwillingness to confront their difficulty. As important as it is for chemically dependent persons to recognize their problem, it is also important that their families, friends, and fellow workers learn about the problem and help the alcoholics deal with it.

Do you know Jim or Mary or Ralph or Esther or Ken? If you suspect that you do, you will want to read *I'm Worried About Your Drinking,* the story of the feelings of people who are troubled because someone they love is drinking too much. Their feelings run the gamut from sympathy and desire to protect to anger and fear.

The struggles of these people are, in many ways, my own. My father had a drinking problem throughout most of my childhood and youth. I worried and despaired. Sometimes I was angry and at other times I denied my feelings or the reality that our family had a problem. I have also felt deep concern for other friends and relatives who are caught up in confusion over alcoholic illness. It is not easy.

As you read this book, experience its feelings. Are they like yours? Is this what is happening to you or to someone you care about? Are you indecisive and concerned? The intent of this book is to help you clarify your feelings and problems. Then it may be possible to look at some alternatives and solutions.

JUDITH MATTISON

CONFUSION

Confusion

I try anger
    but he gives back anger—
    stinging, harsh—
    until I weep.
So I try shame.
    He feels remorse
    and hangs his head
    until he has another drink.
I try pleading,
threats I cannot follow through on.
    He ignores my words
    and I am shamed.
I try drinking with him
    and I am degraded.
I try silence.
And when I'm most resentful
I try ridicule
    and I choke
    on my bitter gall.

I was convinced
that somehow I would find a way
to solve, to change his problem.
But deep inside I know that
it is I who has begun to change.
I live in fear,
discouraged.
I tangle my resolve—
try to please
until frustration tears my smile
in shreds of pain.
I am desperate as I lose
not only his companionship,
but my concept of myself as well.

Rehearsal

I practice my lines.
I intend to be rational.
I shall talk with you
reasonably
about how you are hurting us
and especially yourself
in this abuse.
But when you're well
it's hard to talk about unpleasantness.
And when I find you out of control
my angry disappointment
demolishes my plan for rationality.
You seem to know
when I will be unable to confront you,
and behave accordingly.

Slip

Why!?
Why does she do this?
Everything had gone so well.
We had happy days
        almost a year
        relaxed
        (well, sometimes).
She was cross
and sometimes tense,
but dry.
Now from nowhere
one drink
and she's worse than ever.
I don't understand.
Just when I had let myself
believe that she could manage,
she begins again.
Why?
She meant to change!
Now I have to start all over—
helping.

Sleepless

I lie awake
unsure of what to do.
Your sleep is heavy,
drugged,
and I'm afraid for you.
My eyes burn
and my head is cloudy,
as if I too
had sought my peace
in pills.
Your mornings
must be midnight gray.
You seem to dread
tomorrow.
My concern and my confusion
give me no rest from today
and I lie
awake.

Too young

He's too young to be an alcoholic.
Drinking is a grown-up problem.
Kids just like a beer bust,
showing off from time to time.
But they tell me he's been drinking
every day for months,
even in the morning.
Not enough to notice,
just enough to make the day
more bearable. It scares me.
He seems too young to be an alcoholic.

Compulsion

You tell me you can quit.
You decide to drink—
it is not a question
of compulsion.
You claim that you are
capable of choosing.
Why then
do you choose always
to drink
and choose never
to say no?

Simple

I have watched the soap operas.
People seem to conquer their dependence.
They get well.
Something happens—
good luck—
and the need for chemical escape
seems to disappear.
I keep searching
for that something,
for that luck,
the little change that I can make
to cause a change in you.
Perhaps the scripts on television
make solutions far too simple.
Perhaps there is no easy way.
I wish the scripts were true!

My child

A parent can't help
but wonder.
Is there something I've done
 or not done?
Did I love too little
 too intensely?
Do you drink
to show rebellion?
Or have chemicals become
 less choice,
 more addiction?
I toss at night
afraid,
wondering
 whether to speak
 what to say
 who to tell.
I have, for so long,
been the strong one in your life.
Never before have I felt
so weak.

Speechless

You misunderstand.
I try to say it carefully, but
you proclaim
that you don't need any help.
You don't have a problem!
I wilt beside your power.
There seems nothing I can say
that you do not deny
or attack.
I weaken
and retreat.
Sadness and frustration
fill my throat until
I have nothing left to say.

Indirect

I jab at you a bit.
Comments like
"I see you're ahead of me"
when you've had two drinks to my one.
I wonder aloud
if you've spent all our vacation money
on your favorite wines,
or I offer you a breath mint
in front of the others
at a party.
It's all I can think to do
when my resentment
is edged with embarrassment
or fear.

Playing

Have you noticed?
When the children
in the neighborhood
play house
our son always
tells his "wife"
that they will not have
whiskey in their home.
It makes me proud
and sad.

Consolation

Sometimes
when she's had too much—
too many pills,
too many drinks—
she's warm
and cozy
like she was so long ago.
It feels good
and makes me think
that maybe things will all work out
someday.

Chill

We went along so normally,
one martini every day
at six o'clock,
relaxing before dinner.
Then it changed.
You wanted two.
and then you needed three
to feel relaxed and easy.
One day I realized
that we weren't talking—
you were drinking
silently.
We were alone
together,
and I was chilled
by the unknown
and by an unexplained
and aching sense of dread.

SELF-PITY

Martyr

It's hard to live this way,
day to day,
never knowing how I'll find you,
wondering if the children
will be hungry.
But I tell myself
and all my friends
that I'll be patient,
and I guess that sometimes
life is not a bed of roses.
(They admire my sacrifice.)
I'll carry on
in spite of all my trials.

Silence

I hide my tears.
They soak my pillow
silently.
You hurt me so,
but I will not harass you
and I refuse to beg.
I can only wait
and try to smooth things
for the children.
How long must
I wait
in silence.

Loneliness

When was the last time I felt sure—
confident that you'd be home for dinner
or that tomorrow we could
plan to visit neighbors?
When was it that you
took me for a walk
or brought me flowers
as a gift and not a bribe?
It is years since we went out to dinner
without unspoken fears that
you'd be drunk
before we left for home.
I miss the dinners and the walks.
I miss your company.
I miss your self-reliance.
I know that I am feeling
sorry for myself
but my life has come to be
intolerably lonely.

Tired

I'm so tired.
I try so hard
to hold our family together,
working 'til I'm weary
making decisions we should share.
Winter rains go on and on.
Watering my spirit.
Cold
Lonely
Endless fatigue.

Normal

All these years
I've thought we were a
normal family.
I've begun to look at other families
and compare them with our own.
We are different.
Something's missing—
    openness
    honesty
    feelings.
We don't live naturally
as they do.
We are unpredictable
and cautious,
unsure of each other.
I wish we felt free
    to hug and laugh,
    talk and be ourselves
    and tell the truth.
I wish we knew
what it is to be a family.

ANGER

After school

I never hurry home from school.
I never know
if you'll be out in the kitchen cooking
or in front of television
with a cigarette and highball
and that corny
"Hello dear, how was your day?"
slurring out of your smelly mouth.
One day I poured the bourbon
down the sink.
You didn't say a word,
and after I got over being angry
I felt guilty.
I keep wishing
I could stay in school
all day
all year.

Hate

I hate you
standing there,
rocking in a stupor.
You can't even keep your balance
without effort.
I hate your smile.
It's foolish!
I can't trust that smile
to be warm when I need comfort
or to listen when I tell you
how distraught I feel.
I despise this person
who cannot hold a glass
in confidence,
but rubs the sides
as if to be assured
the hand has feeling—
when the wine has long since
blurred the feelings
and the eyes.
I hate this person
who has no control
over life
or liquor,
but chooses
to ignore the problem
and to torture me.
I hate you when you're drinking!

Robbery

Today my daughter
cried before she left for school
because she cannot have
a simple dress she longs to have.
You spend our money
on your insecurities
and she pays the bitter price
of sacrifice.
You are a thief!
Your family, your victims!

Parenting

My life is backward.
You are my parent.
I should be able to lean on you,
come to you for help,
feel secure.
But you're undependable.
You need me
to find you when you're missing,
cover up your mistakes,
pretend that I like you.
Don't you see,
I don't bring friends home
because you act so infantile
when you're drunk.
No, I don't think you see yourself
as others do.
I don't think you want to.
You prefer this topsy-turvy world.

Wondering

I was wondering the other day
if there ever was a time
when I could trust you.
When I was very small,
did you act predictably?
Did I like to sit on your lap?
Did your breath smell fresh?
It would have been
so nice to know you then.
All I can recall
is the salty liquored smell
of favorite taverns,
juke boxes and peanuts,
the school concerts you missed,
and the time you got sick
all over me.

Resentment

I've been an adult for a hundred years,
doing dishes you should do,
fixing dinners,
cleaning up.
Missing all the fun
because we never know how well you'll be.
You are sick,
always sick.
It's not fair!
I resent the hours
and the worries.
Let me live my life
free of your dependence.
You're not fair!

Celebrations

I hate holidays,
family gatherings—
    false calm,
    meaningless conversation,
    tense smiles.
All the while thunderhead
hovers over everyone
waiting for
    a word
    a gesture
    a mysterious mistake
to ignite the great
Explosion,
and you will drink again.

Tension

You quit, you claim.
But you cannot let it go.
You're preoccupied with abstinence,
snapping at the children,
barking out commands,
irritated by small noises or
changes of routines.
Everyone is tense.
You resent your anxiety
over your problem,
and we must pay the price with you.

Plans

We made our plans—
the zoo, the beach, a picnic supper,
everybody
playing together.
We were ready.
But your errand—
you'd be home by noon.

The children cried.
I fed them supper
and read a special story
to salve their disappointment.

Was it such an effort!
Are we such a problem to you?
Is it never possible
to plan
and count on you?
Or will the mirror
always show my face
streaked with tears of disappointment?

Christmas

I hate Christmas.
All the billboards
filled with cheer
and gin and beer.
Parties,
never knowing how you'll be.
Choking food at lavish tables.
Watching you waver
when you thank the hostess.
Arguing that I must drive.
Hoping you won't take the first one
Christmas Eve.

Family

I'm most angry with them.
I can't fly in fury
at your illness,
hateful as you are when you are drunk.
But they—
if they would only read!
If they would try
to comprehend without histrionics.
To balance their desire to love you
with honest confrontation.
To turn protection
into genuine attempts for change.
To recognize how they could
affect your behavior
without usurping
your responsibility for yourself.

Buddies

Your friends disgust me.
They want you to drink.
They laugh at crude jokes
told in taverns
in semidarkness
where you all get together.
They bring you home
like kindly fathers, but
laugh behind your back
about your drinking
at the football games.
Now and then they claim concern.
They say you might be
having trouble handling the stuff.
But on bowling night
or Saturdays
they always call to see if you can
join them—
and ask you to bring a six pack if you can.

PROTECTION

Secrets

I can't tell his boss.
He might lose his job.
A man can't get along
without a job.
And his friends—
it's so embarrassing.
I'd really rather stay at home.
I try to compensate;
the children miss their daddy,
and sometimes when he drinks too much
it frightens them.
Someday he'll change—
I'll just believe in him
'til then.

Cover-up

They all know.
I try to cover up for you—
telling them you've had a trying day,
chuckling or laughing at you,
trying to appear at ease,
making light of awkward moments.
Still, I'm sure they know
you drink too much.
My masquerades do not disguise
your loss of control.
You're the only one
who doesn't seem to know.
You run away from the reality
of your drinking problem
by drinking.

Excuses

We've tried them all,
dental appointments
	when you're late to work
upset stomachs—mine, the children's—
	when you're hung over
and the old favorite—
you're asleep
	and can't come
	to meet the guest
	or answer the phone.
We do it to "help" you.
Most of them know
it's just a front.
And all it seems to help you do
is drink.
Worst of all,
you honestly believe that you have no problem
and that the excuses are real!

Stricken

Sometimes I think it would be easier
if you were hateful, mean.
Then I'd leave.
I couldn't bear to be abused.
But you're seldom belligerent—
you're pitiful,
sometimes humorous,
even gentle now and then.
You only hit me once.
I swore
you'd never come near me again.
But you cried so in the morning.
I couldn't leave you
desolate like that.

Sympathy

Long ago I gave up shouting.
I think you almost liked the shouting.
You knew what to do with punishment.
You felt sorry for yourself.
But talking doesn't help either.
Today I failed again
because I couldn't say
what I really felt.
You didn't fight back at my words
and I softened.
I forgot to remind you of
the empty bottles in the garage
or the way you fell outside the door.
I didn't recall your sulking quiet
or your angry outburst at the children.
Because you seemed repentant,
I stopped talking.
I believed in willpower again.
I believed your promises.
I failed.
I forgot
you have no power of will
over this disease.

FEAR

Afraid

Please don't hurt yourself.
You drink too much.
You don't eat well.
You shouldn't drive
(you'll kill yourself) and
I'm so afraid for you.
Worst of all, your quiet scares me—
when you hide
behind sullen despondency.
I beg you not to hurt yourself.

Leaving

I tell myself
I can't leave you.
A family needs both parents,
and I keep hoping
I can help you change.

I can't leave you.
You threaten us—
you'll hurt us
you'll self-destruct
you'll tell everyone
it's not your fault
but ours,
and they might believe you.

I can't leave
because I'm not sure
I can survive alone.

I can't leave
because leaving seems to blame you.
Or it signifies
that something's truly wrong,
and I don't want to admit
I've failed.

Relatives

I'd hate to bring it up.
The family couldn't handle this.
If we talked about your problem
I'm not sure what they might do.
They might say or do things
that would only make you worse,
and I would have to live with you that way.
Then sometimes I wonder.
By protecting them from your disease
I may be really hurting you.

Reputation

I can't bear to tell a soul.
People don't understand.
They'll think she's weak.
Her reputation—
all the talk will ruin her
and me.

And telling friends—
humiliation.
They may think
that I'm to blame
or just exaggerating.

I want to help her,
but I can't bear
to tell a soul.

Conflict

I hate conflict.
I'm uncomfortable with arguments
(and you seem to win them all).
Discussions are fraught with tension.
I feel uneasy and incompetent.
My fear of heat
keeps me from the flame of confrontation.
I'm protecting myself from fire,
yet I feel as if
we're burning
with no way of escape.

Gradual

It was a gradual change
from unpleasant
to frightening
to terrible.
Small episodes
changed to outrage
but your apologies
gave me hope.
Now I'm mired
in a problem
and I don't know
when it began
or where to turn.

ANALYSIS

Self-hate

She's grown accustomed to her gray world—
to the clouds.
Punishing herself,
living in remorse and guilt.
She's comfortable in sadness
and in self-abuse,
so she chooses
to relate to the world
in ways which are familiar—
disrespecting her body,
hating her past,
hiding from the future.
She escapes the possibility of growth
by numbing her reality,
and welcomes joy
only when she senses, secretly,
that it will turn to pain.
She's grown accustomed to a cloudy world—
unreal, gray, and dying.

Strength

Grandpa said we must be strong.
Fortitude is the only way.
To stray,
to let ourselves admit our need
would be to bleed
and not to conquer wounds.

We grow up believing
only strength is acceptable.
We must not be weak.
We must prevail.
And so we cannot recognize
that we are overcome.
That would be weakness, don't you see?
"Not me. I'm strong."
And as long as we deny
our need,
we must pretend that we are well,
and can't admit our sickness.

Mother

All his life
she fed him liquor
in empty glasses—
reminding him
when he failed her expectations,
or in quiet actions that said:
"Let me help you.
You need me.
You're irresponsible
but I'll protect you."

So he grew up to a
child-man,
thinking, "I can't do it.
I need help.
You will have to help me
because I don't manage well.
(Mother always said so.)
If someone doesn't help me
I may not survive.
I may decide to succumb—
and it would be your fault
unless you help me."

Guilt

It must be me.
Somehow I have failed her.
I know she felt discouraged
when the kids were small
and I was always working late.
I tried to say I loved her
but she seemed to throw away affection.
Sometimes she was so withdrawn.
Talking didn't help—
she'd close the door.
Her brother doesn't understand.
Her parents won't believe it.
I'm stricken when I wonder
if it's something I do
that causes her to drink this way.
I have no solutions.
She refuses to discuss the problem.
I can only pray to God
it isn't me.

Self-deception

Today you drank.
It does not matter why.
The illness *is*
that it no longer matters why you drink.
The illness is
that you simply can no longer choose not to drink,
you must drink.
And so you destroy
    your family
    the holiday fun
    your self-respect,
slain on an altar of
self-deception.
As long as you claim health
your sickness spreads disease
everywhere you go.
And you are your primary victim.

Weekends

Weekdays are normal.
Irritations magnify,
but you're dry
'til Friday.
By Saturday
it seems to me
you've tried to fail—
as soon as no one
watches you.
Your job is your
custodian.
Without your work
you might not wait to drink
'til Friday.
I wonder if the day will come
when Friday seems
too far away,
then Thursday
and then Wednesday.
Who will watch you then?

Try!

Somewhere you learned to be this way.
Somehow life has taught you
that you cannot cope—
that escape is preferable
to knowledge or decision.
Sometime you decided to try
to put others in your service
rather than to claim strength of your own.

You could choose to risk—
daring to seek success
by acknowledging failure.
You could be willing
to experience life in full—
sorrow, honesty, foolishness,
power, weakness, and joy.
Take a chance on yourself!
You can do it!
Try!

Crazy

When I talk with you
or plead,
trying to help you understand
how you're hurting us,
yourself—
you stare at me
and act as if you think I'm crazy.

Am I?
Am I crazy
to think you're ill,
in need of help?
I doubt my own convictions
when you look or speak like that.
Am I crazy?

Analysis

Does it ever matter why?
I have analyzed
and tried to understand.
But even if I know
you do not change.

DESPAIR

Dissonance

It was a dissonant chord
played firmly
fingers dragged across the keys.
A sighing body
heavy breathing
seething sickly
reeling in the night.
Here was illness
cloaked in chemicals
thudding through the darkness
enveloping the light
leaving only putrid air
and fear
and the dismal sound
of mourning.

Nightmare

Her eyes.
I see it in her eyes.
One sip.
How can a person
be so weak,
so unable to control. . . .
I see it in her eyes.
It starts again—
the nightmare.

Trapped

I love him!
Why do you insist
that I should leave this man?
I know he is disgusting
and it makes me sick
to see him throw away
his capabilities, his skills.
But leaving him
is just as hard
as staying.

Suicide

Every time I hear a television newscast,
read a newspaper report
about a suicide,
my stomach aches
or my fingers clench
and I have to try to change
the subject of my thoughts.
Deep inside I'm afraid
that you'll kill yourself someday.
Worst of all
is my fear
that I'm unable to prevent it.

Taxi driver

The taxi driver brought you home,
helped you up the stairs and into the house,
where you stumbled against the piano
and fell.
There was no money in the house
to pay the driver,
and you were broke.
All the money I had in those days
was a piggy bank full of pennies.
I got the bank
and counted out the pennies for the man
as I cried.
You don't remember, of course.
Your blackout system is your escape.
As I look back,
it isn't the tears or the pennies
or your stumbling and threats
that I remember most.
It's the kind, but helpless look,
the sad sympathy extended to me
in the taxi driver's eyes.

Hospital

The hospital again.
It's all that I can do
to dress and put my hands on
the steering wheel
which takes me to you.
Yesterday you lay on the front seat,
a sick and crying child
in need of help.
I was driven by my fear,
forced by your wanton
neglect of your own welfare.
I was driven to the choice
of taking you to the alien
hospital.
Now I dread the moment
when I see you
lying helpless in that bed.
Sick—
your body weak in its withdrawal,
your pallid face
and sunken eyes
too ashamed to look at me
in honest morning light.
Tears well in my eyes
to know how painful
every morning confrontation is for you.
I can only pray
someday
you'll bear the morning—
find the strength to make it
all the day and night
without relying on
the company and fortitude
of drinking.

Fears

I feel desperate
when you aren't here.
It isn't quite so hard
when I have someone else to talk with.
But left alone,
I visualize you
driving wildly down the highway,
meeting someone else
at a tacky bar,
or trusting someone who will
take advantage
of your inability to reason.
I have no control over you.
I can only wait
and hope.

Loss

What has happened
to the happy friend
I used to have—
who laughed with me
and loved good fun.
We hardly get together anymore.
The happy friend
abandoned me
and living.
Only a shadow
stays behind—
a quiet shadow
laughing like an echo,
strained.
Always drinking,
hesitant and distant.
I miss my friend.

Eggshells

Life becomes intolerable.
Waiting,
dreading,
walking on chalk eggshells
only to be hurt again.
I'd rather die
than live another day
in this despair.

AVOIDANCE

Someday

I kept thinking he would change.
I knew he was a rounder.
But after we were married. . . .

I kept thinking he felt insecure.
I would simply have to love him more.
A little more time. . . .

I kept thinking he needed more to live for.
A baby would be such a joy.
When the baby came. . . .

I kept thinking he would realize.
He's not the kind of person
who would hurt his family. . . .

I kept thinking someone else
would say the words,
if I would only wait. . . .

I kept thinking,
someday. . . .

Accusations

It seems such an accusation—
calling anyone an alcoholic—
especially when we're not certain.
We have problems, yes.
And alcohol is often part of
our dilemma.
But to *say* it.
It's like a brand somehow—
a shame, perhaps.
Or worse, if we should say it,
we might have to face the fact
it's true.

Barroom conversation

Russ drinks like a trooper.
He blames it on his wife—
"Never satisfied, that woman."
'Course it ain't so easy
when Russ doesn't show on Friday night
and she's got no money for the morning milk.
Funny fellow, Russ.
Nice guy.
Man, he'd give his shirt away
if you wuz needin' it.
He just can't drink that stuff.
But you can't go over there
and talk to him.
He ain't gonna listen,
or he'll tell ya
that he only drinks on weekends
or that his woman is a shrew.

Hey—you!
You can't go over there!
Can you?

Daytime

It frightens me
because I've been there
early Monday morning
and I know her coffee cup
is filled with more than coffee.
I wonder what she's thinking.
And I worry when, at two o'clock,
her shades are still drawn shut.
She must feel awfully lonely.
And it doesn't seem right
that she stays indoors
in darkness
by herself
nearly every day.
I try to be a friend.
But I wouldn't dream of asking. . . .
I wouldn't pry.
Still, I feel so sad for her.
Do you think that I should try?

Friends

Cathy shouldn't drink so much.
Roger either.
But after all,
we all have one or two too many
now and then.
Anyway
how could we say . . .
I mean,
what do you say to friends
who drink too much?
We'd hate to leave them out, and
we surely can't expect the rest
to sacrifice their fun
because two friends
can't handle liquor like the others.
Here, Cathy, let me help you to the car.
Roger, have another.

Consequences

We won't mention
that your name is in the paper
for a drunken driving charge—
the seventh time.
(The seventh time!
How often must this happen
before you'll admit that
you can't control your habit?)
We hope that
Grandma won't see it.
And we won't talk about it
because you'll only snap at us
the rest of the afternoon.

Rationalizing

We mustn't let him hurt himself.
Deep inside we know he's good—
    a kind man
    generous and smiling
    prone to dream a bit
    but good.
He can't help himself.
If we don't make excuses for him,
he may have to face his choices.
He may look at what he does
and hate himself,
or worse,
continue to destroy himself
(or me!)
I'd rather bolster his despair
    a little fib
    encouragement
    a dollar or a half-truth here or there.
Some day, who knows,
perhaps he'll want to change.

Miracles

They're waiting for a miracle—
a great inheritance, perhaps,
or some deep, solemn moment
when the truth will bare itself
like gleaming noon sun,
striking down a lifelong pattern
of self-despair or degradation, drinking.
Some shining day,
a fairy-tale solution.
They dream a day when
a person who has learned to cope with life
by denying its reality
will, without apparent cause,
like a majestic mystery,
change
from dying to living.
A miracle.

Skid row

I watch the men on skid row.
(Where do the drinking women go?)
They look so cold in winter wind,
coats too long, scrubby beards,
fumbling hands and feet.
They seem so distant from my life,
living alone and afraid,
unable to handle life.

Then I look at our lives.
Alone at parties,
afraid of sobriety,
fumbling everything but jobs
in the cold of indecision
and running away from life.
Standing like children in oversized coats,
unable to move, and overwhelmed.
Not distant from skid row.
Just a different neighborhood,
that's all.

DECISIONS

Believing

You told me you could do it.
I believed in you,
again
and then again—
but you went on.
All the schemes I used
to try to make you change
were worthless.
You went on.

I'm finished trying.
You're the only person
who can choose to change.
You're the one who has to take
an honest look
at who you are
and what you've done.
I can believe in you
if you will take responsibility
for your own life.
Die
or live—
the choice is yours.
If you choose to live,
I'll be beside you.

Choices

Everybody makes a choice
to laugh or cry
to give up or try
to be silent
to complain
to leave
to stay
to face the truth or
to pretend.
You may choose your actions,
and I may choose
to respond with mine.

My change

For years I've made decisions,
carried responsibility
on my own.
I've grown accustomed
to independence.
I didn't ask for your opinion.
I learned to trust myself.

It's hard to change.
Troubled feelings
and our difficulties
are at least familiar.
If you change
what will happen to me?

Glimmer

I have heard of places
where they help dependent people—
help them stop
and somehow begin again.
Rehabilitation.

Self-determination

I have believed
a person must make changes for himself.
I cannot create your happiness.
That is up to you.
Something in your drinking tells me
you can no longer try to change
without my intervention.
Disease has struck—
disease which takes away your choice
to help yourself.
Unless I understand your illness,
show you that it does exist,
hang on to my self-respect
and lead you to honest treatment,
you will not even see
that you need to change.

Confrontation

I'm tired of complaining
and being shocked
and trying to outguess you.
Disappointment treads a weary path—
I'm tired of that, too.
I intend one thing—
to help you face your illness.
I will not harass you.
I will not pretend for you.
I will not desert you.
But I intend to tell you
to show you
to reveal to you and remind you of
the effects of your choices,
the sadness of those who care.
I intend to uncover
the reality you have carefully disguised—
that your behavior is self-destructive.
But I will reassure you
that I care.

Resolve

You mean to quit.
Your resolve is firm.
You can do it, you profess.
Once you quit for seven years
(I remember).
But you fail to recognize
that "to quit" means
every day you stop.
You put away the promises
and choose—
one decision at a time—
to stop,
to cease,
to build on this day and this moment—
not on the seven years, long-drowned,
not on tomorrow
or next weekend.
Your decision happens now
and now
and now.

Rescue

I drove hundreds of miles
in blind rescue attempts
    bringing you home from the tavern
    picking you up at the center
    driving you to the celebration
because we weren't sure
that you were well enough to drive.
I called to make excuses
    too sick to come
    unexpected guests.

I tried to explain
    what would make you act this way
    how your past and present
      caused you to feel as you did.

I went to work,
cared for your health,
cleaned up after you, and
paid your bills.
I did all of this because
I thought you needed me.
I couldn't stand to see you suffering,
feeling unloved, insecure.
My need to ease your tension was as great
as your need to escape or to lean.

Now I realize that in all those rescue attempts,
I never let you take charge of
your own mistakes.
My rescues
kept you drowning.
When I ceased the rescue,
you began to swim.

Harmony

Once
far down the path
I heard a whisper
    small
    but clear.
The voice spoke of better days—
a time when we would
    talk
    and laugh
    and cry together,
    glad to know it all.
The message made me cry.
The sound became a song
    now loud
    fading
    then returning,
drawing me to seek
the source.
The melody repeats.
There is an answer
if I will only follow
the sound of caring
to help.

Conclusion

It may very well be that the disease of chemical dependency has affected you and your loved ones. You are not alone. You are not peculiar. You are not to blame.

If you have experienced the feelings expressed in *I'm Worried About Your Drinking,* there is something you can do. Reach out for help. Find out what you can do about your troubles and confusion. Call or write:

- a local Al-Anon group
- a local Alcoholics Anonymous group
- Johnson Institute, 10700 Olson Memorial Highway, Minneapolis, Minnesota 55441; 612-544-4165.
- Hazelden Foundation, Box 11, Center City, Minnesota 55012; 800-328-9288 (toll free).

I know you feel afraid or hesitant. But for your own health and for the sake of the drinking person, reach out for information and help.

Basic facts about alcoholism

1. Alcoholism is a disease. Alcoholics cannot choose not to drink. They feel that they must drink and they construct their lives to achieve that end.

2. Alcoholism is not curable. It is possible to arrest the disease, and to treat it. But unless the person ceases drinking and receives treatment, the disease gets progressively worse and is eventually terminal. Alcoholism is chronic.

3. Everyone who is close to the chemically dependent person is affected by the disease. Often friends and loved ones develop patterns of coping with the disease which are not helpful in solving the problem.

4. Ten million Americans are alcoholics. The Health, Education, and Welfare Department considers alcoholism to be our number one health problem.

5. Alcoholics deny that drinking causes their problems. They tend to project their difficulties onto others.

6. Judging, blaming, pleading, and scolding are ineffective in dealing with the chemically dependent person.

7. There is hope! If someone who is important to the dependent person will intervene in a nonjudgmental way, confronting the dependent with the facts of their dilemma, it is possible for the dependent to seek and receive help. You can learn about intervention. Write or call one of the groups listed on page 103. They are successful in helping with chemical dependency problems.